Hope
And Other Life Seasonings

Hope
And Other Life Seasonings

Cathy Burnham Martin

Published and printed in the United States of America

www.QTPublishing.com

Quiet Thunder Publishing
Naples, FL   Manchester, NH   Columbus, NC

**This title and more can be found at
www.GoodLiving123.com**

Copyright © 2025 Quiet Thunder Publishing
Naples, FL   Manchester, NH   Columbus, NC

All rights reserved worldwide. No part of this book may be reproduced in any form or by any means without prior written permission from the publisher or authors, except for the inclusion of brief quotations embodied in critical essays, articles, or reviews. These articles and/or reviews must state the correct title and author by name.

Paperback edition: ISBN 978-1-939220-64-6
eBook edition: ISBN 978-1-939220-65-3
Audiobook edition: ISBN 978-1-939220-68-4

Library of Congress Control Number: 2025914253

Dedication

"Hope" is lovingly dedicated to everyone who has taken the time and perspicacity to lift the spirits of someone else in need, to help them see the sun despite the clouds, and to teach the means to face adversity with positivity and action. We need more sweet souls in this world just like you.

I especially recognize my husband in dedicating "Hope." Throughout his struggles with cancer, followed by a stroke, hope was not always close at hand for him. When Life feels the most bleak, keeping hope alive can literally keep our bodies alive. I immensely respect you, Sir Ronald, for passing through the ups and downs of these dreadfully challenging times with as much hope burning or even flickering as you could. You and hope both live to pay it forward. God bless.

Hope

Foreword

As part of my ongoing research in life, I continually seek out and collect quips, quotations, words of wisdom, serious thoughts, and humorous tidbits. These "Notable Quotables" hail from all walks of life, the famous and the lesser known, both modern and classically aged. I share some of these gems to add sparkle to our thinking and support in times when harmony is deeply needed.

> *"The wisdom of the wise and the experience of the ages are perpetuated by quotations."*
> --Benjamin Disraeli (1804-1881)
> British statesman &
> Prime Minister of the United Kingdom

(Photo by Xander Lacy)

Hope is among the most precious of Life's seasonings, as it opens doors, builds our fortitude, and lets light shine into some of the darkest places and times. When we need a sparkle of hope, let this be a treasured Go-To guide.

> *"No winter lasts forever;*
> *no spring skips its turn."*
> —Hal Borland (1900 – 1978)
> American writer & journalist

May we always hold hope close to our hearts and strengthen it in others. May our constant evolution continue.

Table of Contents

Dedication	v
Foreword	vii
1 Defining Hope	1
2 Recognizing Relevance	7
3 Overcoming Despair	13
4 Practicing Gratitude	23
5 Visualizing Positive	31
6 Taking Action	39
7 Nurturing	49
8 Celebrating	57
9 Worksheets	67
10 In Closing	75
Photography Credits	79
About the Author	81
Other Titles	83
Partial List of Audiobooks Narrated by Cathy Burnham Martin	87

Hope

Table of Contents

(Photo by Joshua Earle)

Defining Hope

"Hope is the power of being cheerful in circumstances which we know to be desperate."

-- G.K. Chesterton (1882 - 1945)
English author, philosopher, & journalist

According to the Oxford dictionary, hope is "an expectation and desire for certain things to happen." Merriam-Webster defines hope slightly differently, stating hope is "to cherish a desire with anticipation." Spiritually, hope is a confidant expectation that is rooted in faith, specifically faith in God, a higher power or a divine plan.

"Hope is the companion of power, and mother of success; for who so hopes strongly has within him the gift of miracles."

-- Samuel Smiles (1812 - 1904)
British author & government reformer

Hope

Unlike basic optimism, hope is based on a deep-seated belief. While optimism paints with a broad brush, hope is a highly focused pinpoint.

*"Hope is definitely not
the same thing as optimism.
It is not the conviction that
something will turn out well,
but the certainty that
something makes sense,
regardless of how it turns out."*

-- Václav Havel (1936 - 2011)
Czech statesman, author, & dissident
Last president of Czechoslovakia (1989 - 1992)

(Photo by Ahmed Hasan)

Hope is all about motivation, resilience, positive outlook, overcoming adversity, dealing with unknowns, reaching desired outcomes, managing stress and anxiety, and allowing us to believe that recovery is possible. We can overcome challenges.

It all starts with motivation, which reflects the influence of our internal or external driving forces. We may be inspired by pure enjoyment. Perhaps we are encouraged to keep on going with a project because it gives us a true sense of purpose. External motivators could include a monetary reward, possible promotion at work, awards, or some other special recognition.

Often, what motivates us are things we cannot see. Though very different factors and forces motivate different people, we all need some sort of stimulation to be encouraged to keep moving forward, especially when the going gets tough.

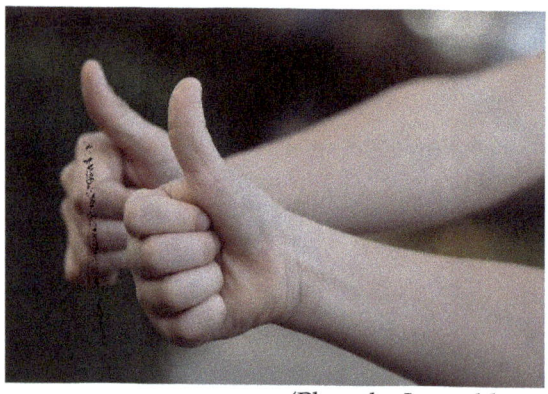

(Photo by Leopold Boettcher)

(Photo by Siegfried Poepperl)

"Hope is the thing with feathers
That perches in the soul
And sings the tune without the words
And never stops
At all."

-- Emily Dickinson (1830 - 1886)
American poet

Hope can be more than just an elusive motivating factor. I've even heard hope spoken of as a healthy, long-lasting antidote in our divisively chaotic world.

Some potentially crazy verbal conflicts do seem to pop up almost daily. Without the intervention of hope, we could find our hearts and spirits deeply wounded.

> *"Hope is both the earliest*
> *and the most indispensable virtue*
> *inherent in the state of being alive.*
> *If life is to be sustained*
> *hope must remain,*
> *even where confidence is wounded,*
> *trust impaired."*
>
> -- Erik H. Erikson (1902 - 1994)
> German American child psychoanalyst
> & visual artist

Hope is vital for building and rebuilding our resiliency. When hopeful, we are far more likely to bounce back and bounce back much more quickly.

> *"The grand essentials to happiness in this life are something to do, something to love, and something to hope for."*
>
> -- Joseph Addison Richard Steele (1672 -1719)
> British writer & politician

2

<u>Recognizing Relevance</u>

*"He who has health, has hope.
And he who has hope, has everything."*

-- Arabian Proverb

(Photo by Christo Anestev)

No one argues against the fact that hope reduces depression. Even when we are not "down," hope can swiftly lower our stress levels. When we are feeling more positive mentally, our physical health is also boosted.

*"There is no medicine like hope,
no incentive so great,
and no tonic so powerful
as expectation of something tomorrow."*

-- Orison Swett Marden (1848 - 1924)
American author & publisher
Founder of "Success" magazine

(Photo by Demiahl)

When we have the positivity of hope, we become better collaborators with other people, too. Hope enhances problem solving during extreme and daily challenges. When we allow ourselves to believe, hope provides a solution-focused mindset.

Recognizing Relevance

(Photo by J. Avard)

*"Of all the forces that make for a better world,
none is so indispensable,
none so powerful,
as hope.
Without hope men are only half alive.
With hope they dream and think and work."*

-- Charles Henry Sawyer (1868 - 1954)
American artist & photographer

Hope

When obstacles appear to have blocked all avenues and thwarted all possible efforts, we need hope. Hope gives us clarity. Hope helps us navigate obstacles with both creative thinking and determination of purpose. Hope boosts our confidence and can-do thinking.

*"The enjoyment of life would be instantly gone
if you removed
the possibility of doing something."*

-- Chauncey Mitchell Depew (1834 - 1928)
American attorney, businessman, & politician

(Photo by Nick Fewings)

Recognizing Relevance

(Photo by Everton Vila)

Hopeful people build better and more positive relationships. When we are hopeful, people are drawn to us and want to work with us or socialize with us. With hope, we foster stronger, long-lasting relationships.

*"Men and women are limited
not by the place of their birth,
not by the color of their skin,
but by the size of their hope."*

-- John H. Johnson (1918 - 2005)
American businessman & publisher
Founder "Ebony" magazine

Hope adds valuable meaning to our lives and helps us to look forward positively. Life is not just about today. When we hope, we also prepare for even brighter tomorrows. Hope is a beautiful form of inspiration.

> *"Without hope,*
> *we cannot survive,*
> *much less progress."*

-- Warren G. Bennis (1925 - 2014)
American scholar, author, & consultant

(Photo by Hayley Murray)

Overcoming Despair

"Extreme hopes are born from extreme misery."

-- Bertrand Russell (1892 - 1970)
British philosopher, logician, & intellectual

We all may wish that we could hold positive attitudes every day. However, Life can overflow with angst, suffering, and hardship, sometimes far more frequently than anyone would wish. These are the very challenges that teach us to develop and hold fast to hope. Remember the age-old advice for when we've reached the end of our rope. "Tie a knot and hang on!" These are the exact times when we can and need to develop the power of hope.

"Hope begins in the dark, the stubborn hope that if you just show up and try to do the right thing, the dawn will come. You wait and watch and work: you don't give up."

-- Anne Lamott (1954 -)
American novelist

(Photo by Annie Spratt)

When we learn of someone else being in the throes of despair, we may feel helplessly inadequate to be of any help. And yet, just acknowledging their suffering is important. This does not mean trying to assure someone with statements like, "Everything happens for a reason" or "Everything will be fine" or "Things eventually work themselves out."

This does not always happen. Such statements can feel "empty," though filled with well-intentioned positivity. Sadly, not everything will have a happy ending. Sometimes we must learn to deal more positively with a very negative scenario. Tragedy is part of our lives.

Genuine empathy cannot take away someone else's grief, but it can deeply help someone to know that they are not alone. We are there for them. They have a right to feel exactly as they are feeling.

And we never know, perhaps our gentle words or our hand reaching out to hold theirs can also revive their sense of hope, exactly when they need it most. No matter how small we may feel, we are never powerless. Sometimes, we just need to try.

> *"Just as despair can come to one*
> *only from other human beings,*
> *hope, too,*
> *can be given to one*
> *only by other human beings."*

-- Elie Wiesel (1928 - 2016)
Romanian American author, Nobel Prize winner,
& Holocaust survivor

Despite our best efforts, there can still be times when we struggle to hang onto hope. Some of these times are those when, for example, constant pain and suffering have sapped every last bit of strength and patience we think we can possibly muster up. It becomes difficult to even imagine that a current situation or feeling is not our "new normal" and will plague us forever.

Separating ourselves from positivity when we are "down" is very important to avoid. Isolation is not a comfortable place, and it is not related to happy "alone times" when we may seek privacy and quiet.

"Alone time" is a happy place. Isolation is purely desolate and negative.

Isolation separates us from every positive person, sensation, opportunity, or influence. In isolation we can find ourselves on a downward, self-critical, vicious cycle. Isolation fuels cruel despair and misplaced feelings of unworthiness.

(Photo by Sasha Freemind)

This is the opposite impact we want. We want to nurture our well-being and sense of worthiness. We need to communicate with supportive, genuinely caring people and focus on positives.

No matter how illogical it may sound at the time, we also need to remind ourselves that feeling despair is temporary, not permanent. We can seek words for our despair and our healing through poets, music, or writers. Acknowledging our despair reduces its power over us.

"Hope is the feeling you have that the feeling you have isn't permanent."

-- Jean Kerr (1922 - 2003)
American author & playwright

Hope is linked with good health and happiness. We all hope for both, though we may not have yet developed healthy or happy habits.

With chronic illness, hope helps us enjoy better coping skills. Even in the very worst scenarios, hope is a powerful companion. For example, hope can help us find comfort and even joy in terminal health situations.

> *"When you think about it,*
> *what other choice is there but to hope?*
> *We have two options,*
> *medically and emotionally:*
> *Give up or fight like hell."*
>
> -- Lance Armstrong (1971 -)
> American professional racing cyclist
> & cancer survivor
> As quoted in "Armstrong's drive,
> decency and inspiration" by Harvey Mackay,
> Arizona Republic, August 15, 2001

Hope literally protects us against depression and suicide. When we feel hopeless is when we need hope restored… and quickly.

(Photo by Gabin Vallet)

While that sounds obvious, it is not easy. What we may need to do is to turn, "Why me?" into "Why <u>not</u> me?" We are just humans. Although different, we are also very much the same. None of us is so special that we will be somehow exempt from calamity, devastation, and heartache.

So, "Why <u>not</u> me?" What might I do or say now that may help someone else who finds themselves in this or another similarly dark place? Even if I feel hopeless for myself, I may well be able to help someone else. Hope is linked with quality of life, self-esteem and a sense of purpose.

"At the darkest moment comes the light."

-- Joseph Campbell (1904 - 1987)
American writer

(Photo by Mohammad Alizade)

To escape from despair, we can focus on recognizing and processing our feelings. We can seek support. We can join in activities that promote our well-being and a positive frame of mind.

At the same time, we need to try not to judge our emotions, regardless of how negative we may be feeling. In fact, it helps to express negative emotions, as long as we do it in healthy ways. We may pick up a notebook and write down our thoughts and feelings. We could talk with a person we sincerely trust. We may even express through a creative outlet, such as some form of art.

Fight the fight. Focus forward. Never give up. Absolutely never give up.

> *"If you lose hope,*
> *you're just not looking far enough ahead."*

-- Joe Tye (1951 -)
American author & poet

(Photo by Ryan Stone)

4

__Practicing Gratitude__

> *"Every cloud has a silver lining, but it is sometimes difficult to get it to the mint."*
>
> -- Don Marquis (1878 - 1937)
> American humorist & journalist

Hope lets us enjoy happiness, but hope often also requires great courage. We can't simply say that we are hoping to believe or to know something.

However, when we develop an attitude of gratitude, we can build hope because we learn to think about all the little things that are good in our lives. No matter how bleak our current moments may feel, some good things have happened, regardless of how tiny they may seem. Practicing gratitude helps us appreciate the positive.

> *"We do not really feel grateful to those who make our dreams come true; they ruin our dreams."*
>
> -- Eric Hoffer (1902 - 1983)
> American philosopher & longshoreman

(Photo by Rosie Kerr)

Practicing gratitude is easier when we create and work to maintain some positive habits. For example, we should prioritize our own physical health. This includes developing good sleeping habits, eating well, and taking part in regular physical activity.

(Photo by Jared Rice)

Another powerful step is including some relaxation techniques in our regular routines. These can be as simple as deep breathing exercises or regular at-home meditation time. We are focusing on where we want to go and better preparing ourselves to get there.

*"Let your hopes, not your hurts,
shape your future."*

-- Robert H. Schuller (1926 - 2015)
American Christian televangelist & author

(Photo by Youngki Son)

These are also times when writing things down or keeping a journal plays an instrumental role in our success. Reflect on positive things that have happened.

If it seems unlikely that anything good has happened that day, think back, regardless of how far. Try to think of 3, 4, or even 5 things each day that are or have been good.

Beyond writing down these positive thoughts, we can and should say, "Thank you" to people who have had an uplifting impact on us. When we think about someone who has had a positive influence on our life, we can share that fact with them. They may be utterly surprised. Regardless, they will find it both humbling and meaningful.

Whether or not we share thoughts, we can write letters of gratitude to various people. Then we can choose whether to send them or not. Sharing our sentiments is great, but not utterly necessary.

(Photo by Nick Morrison)

Sometimes we have completely lost touch with people who have affected us tremendously. Sometimes our influential people are no longer among us.

We should tell the stories to ourselves anyway. We can write our stories in heartfelt letters. Doing this lifts up our own hope. Better yet, if we choose to share them, we may just help someone else, too.

> "*Acknowledging the good that you already have in your life is the foundation for all abundance.*"
>
> --Eckhart Tolle (1948 -)
> German teacher & author

Another little "feel good" activity that I have employed for various purposes is something I will call here a Gratitude Jar. Of course, it could be a Hope Jar, Love Jar, Strength Jar, or designed to suit any uplifting personal need.

Any covered container will work, even a cookie jar. Fill it with little slips of paper containing positive thoughts, things for which we are grateful, quotes that inspire us, uplifting thoughts someone has shared with us.

Daily or anytime that we need a boost, we can walk by the jar and take one out. Reading it will likely bring a much-needed smile to our face.

"Things turn out best for people who make the best of the way things turn out."

--John Wooden (1910 – 2010)
American basketball coach & player

When we are learning to practice an attitude of gratitude, it helps to remind ourselves not to complain. We all likely know someone who seems to get cranky and cross and then moan and groan about virtually anything and anybody.

Experiencing this is tiresome at best and always a serious downer. We want to emulate the positive we observe and admire in other people, but let the negative pass us by.

Regularly practicing gratitude also eliminates any compulsion to compare ourselves with someone else. It is far too easy to look around us and think that someone else or everyone else has it all together. Everything seems to go "right" for them.

Not true. Usually, it just seems that way because we are filled with self-criticism or self-pity. When we practice gratitude, we build resilience against current and future challenges, too.

(Photo by Graddes)

"Hope is the best part of our riches."

-- Christian Nestell Bovee (1820 - 1904)
American writer & epigrammatic

5

<u>Visualizing Positive</u>

(Photo by Majid Akbari)

*"In the factory we make cosmetics;
in the store we sell hope."*

-- Charles Revson (1906 - 1975)
American businessman & philanthropist
Founder of Revlon

Recognize the importance of hope. Hope lifts us, our spirits, and our entire being into a more positive place.

When we can picture ourselves in a better situation, apart from our doubts and enjoying a brighter future, we are positively visualizing. Once we positively visualize, we can start building toward that successful reality.

"Your positive action combined with positive thinking results in success."

– Shiv Khera (1961 -)
Indian author

(Photo by Casey Horner)

Connecting with Nature can also be a very healing experience. If we are in a rural area, taking a walk amongst trees, flowers, and singing birds is easy.

If we are in an urban environment, we may need to become more creative. Seek out a favorite park at sunrise. Or try visiting an arboretum. Sometimes we can do something as seemingly simple as sitting in a window and watching the clouds rolling by or the sky turning colors at sunset.

(Photo by Gavin Spear)

When we let ourselves connect with Nature, we stop any false thinking that we are somehow the center of the Universe. We appreciate the balance and the role we can play.

> *"Today a new sun rises for me;*
> *everything lives,*
> *everything is animated,*
> *everything seems to speak to me of my passion,*
> *everything invites me to cherish it."*

-- Anne Ninon de l'Enclos (1620 - 1705)
French author & courtesan

(Photo by Joshua Earle)

Some people seem to have happy living skills that we may fear we lack. Can we develop such abilities? Oh, yes!

(Photo by Eugene Chystiakov)

We can all learn to be comfortably calm, uncannily upbeat, and purely positive. Looking on the bright side is a choice. Even in a storm, think how delightful it will be to recognize that the sun will return, that the rain will help more flowers grow, and that the discomfort we feel now is not going to last forever.

"Hope is the parent of faith."

-- Cyrus Augustus Bartol (1813 - 1900)
American Unitarian pastor & author

We believe good things will happen when we have faith in a higher power. This is good news. We mere humans are not and do not have to be in control of this planet or this massive thing called Life.

(Photo by Alex Shute)

God may direct our hopes to be expressed through prayer. We can talk, or share with God in ways that make us comfortable. There is no wrong way. This is our personal relationship. We can choose and believe in positive actions, thoughts, and beliefs.

Visualizing Positive

(Photo by Julia Caesar)

"Never talk defeat. Use words like hope, belief, faith, victory."

-- Norman Vincent Peale (1898 - 1993)
American Protestant clergyman & author
From his 1993 book "Positive Thinking Every Day"

We can visualize our personal successes, regardless of how large or small our dreams may be. We can see the results we want in our minds. Only then can we put together a game plan with attainable action steps to reach our goals.

*"Ordinary people believe only in the possible.
Extraordinary people visualize not what is
possible or probable,
but rather what is impossible.
And by visualizing the impossible, they begin
to see it as possible."*

– Chérie Carter-Scott (1949 -)
American author

6

Taking Action

"The future depends on what you do today."

– Mahatma Gandhi (1869 – 1948)
Indian lawyer & political ethicist

Hope is an active choice to make things better. That's simple to say but following up on that choice requires action steps.

I like to start with self-reflection. The more in touch we are with what makes us tick, the more easily we can understand our choices. What are we doing or what is going on around us when we feel the most calm or confident or happy or hopeful? What are the circumstances when we feel the most anxious or insecure or sad or pessimistic?

The next step is identifying what brings us happiness. It is equally important to know what triggers challenging, negative thoughts. We want to be equally aware of both, so we can gain more control over our own lives and attitudes.

(Photo by Corey Hearne)

"Hope for the best but prepare for the worst."

-- English Proverb

As we have discussed, practicing gratitude and visualizing success are important skills in our Hope toolbox. Becoming a person who flourishes with great hope is a process, somewhat like getting our bodies physically healthier.

To reach our goals, we can seek support from and connections with others. We need not just look for guidance, but we can help others who are on similar pathways. Throughout the process, we should continually practice self-care and mindfulness.

Taking Action

> *"Don't wish it were easier; wish you were better."*
>
> -- Jim Rohn (1930 - 2009)
> American entrepreneur & author

When we set goals, there is always the end game... the big goal. It may be set for a year down the road, but it is what we consider to be our primary goal. The biggest challenge with a big goal is that reaching it is a long process. We can get frustrated and demoralized along the way.

(Photo by Julius Drost)

To avoid setbacks and common pitfalls, we need to be sure that all goals, both large and small, are clearly defined. For instance, if I say my goal is to lose weight, the statement is too general. How much weight? A little or a lot? 5 pounds or 20? In a year or a month?

(Photo by Anthony Wade)

In addition to clear specifications, our chances of long-term success are greatly enhanced when we also set various intermediary goals. Depending on the overall goal, these may include daily, weekly, or monthly milestones. Or they may specify certain skills that we will learn and practice as we approach the primary goal.

Breaking big goals into smaller pieces is much the same as a childhood joke that I recall. How do you eat an elephant? 'One bite at a time' was the answer.

"Dream small dreams. If you make them too big, you get overwhelmed and you don't do anything. If you make small goals and accomplish them, it gives you the confidence to go on to higher goals."

– John H. Johnson (1918 – 2005)
American businessman & publisher
Founder "Ebony" magazine

If hope seems to elude our grasp, we may need to regroup. Our tendency might be to hide. However, hope is NOT burying our heads in the sand and simply waiting for changes to take place.

(Photo by Andrey Tikhonovskiy)

Hope is becoming actively involved in encouraging positive changes. We will face ups and downs along the way, but focusing on hope helps us develop resilience and maturity. We <u>can</u> do this, and our success is up to each of us.

> *"Is life so wretched?*
> *Isn't it rather your hands which are too small,*
> *your vision which is too muddled?*
> *You are the one who must grow up."*

>> -- Dag Hammarskjöld (1905 - 1961)
>> Swedish economist & diplomat
>> Secretary-General of the United Nations

(Photo by Joshua Earle)

En route to becoming solidly hopeful people, we help ourselves by improving our habits. These often focus on self-care, as these are the areas we most commonly overlook as we work to take care of other people, tend to our homes and yards, or do our jobs.

Light another spark by pursuing a passion. We often focus on our "Have to Do" lists. Then there may also be the "Need to Do" lists, which are secondary in importance. Most of us completely overlook or don't even write down our "Want to Do" lists.

Let's change that. Let's write down those things we have always wanted to do. Perhaps it was painting a picture or writing a poem or climbing a mountain or singing karaoke or volunteering for a good cause in our communities. We can set our hidden passion free. Give it a try. This is a big part of personal development, and it is very healthy.

Pursuing a passion, regardless of how silly it might be, does not mean we are ignoring or not acknowledging challenges. We are hoping for better. We are helping ourselves to be better, which helps us pursue our goals.

Hope is not a denial of reality. Hope is a realization that just because something is wrong, it does not have to stay that way.

"Prayer is not an old woman's idle amusement. Properly understood and applied, it is the most potent instrument of action."

-- Mahatma Gandhi (1869 - 1948)
Indian lawyer & political ethicist

Importantly, hope is not just a wish. Hope is action oriented. Hope is a skill that can be learned.

"Hope is a talent like any other."

-- Storm Jameson (Margaret Ethel Storm Jameson)
(1891 - 1986)
English journalist & author

(Photo by Oleg Ivanov)

"The only limit to our realization of tomorrow will be our doubts of today."

-- Franklin D. Roosevelt (1882 - 1945)
　　　　　32nd U.S. President

7

Nurturing

*"Spend enough time around
success and failure,
and you learn a reverence for possibility."*

-- Dale A. Dauten (1950 -)
American businessman, innovator, & author

Dad used to say that if we rolled around with pigs we'd come up muddy. I later understood that he wanted us to choose our friends carefully.

Hopeful people are more optimistic, positive, and nurturing. They are not the fanatical types that insist that everyone must believe as they do, since they, obviously, are the only ones with a clue.

Hopeful people believe in us as individuals. That means they respect our individual thoughts and opinions. They do not let their insecurities or personal preferences or issues guide their advice to us. They help us keep encouraged. For success, we should surround ourselves with positivity and let ourselves shine.

"The words that enlighten the soul are more precious than jewels."

-- Hazrat Inayat Khan (1882 - 1927)
Indian philosopher, poet,
& professor of musicology

(Photo by Yanis Ladjouzi)

To grow as positive, hopeful people, we can also focus on activities and media that inspire us and reinforce healthy and helpful behaviors and choices. We need to learn to be cautious of opinion molders who predict doom, downfall, and dreadful consequences for all things with which they disagree. We are all best served by surrounding ourselves with positive, hopeful influences and "influencers."

Nurturing

(Photo by Marko Brecic)

*"Hold up to him his better self,
his real self that can dare and do and win out.
People radiate what is in their minds
and in their hearts."*

-- Eleanor H. Porter (1868-1920)
American novelist
From her 1912 book, "Pollyanna," Chapter 5

Even while we are on our own growth paths, we can still wrap someone else in our arms, look them in the eyes, and tell them that we won't give up. Everyone needs hope.

Hope helps us cope with life's setbacks. These can range from losing jobs, relationships, or family members. We are very vulnerable during and following setbacks.

(Photo by Mark-Olivier Jodoin)

"Hope is always available to us.
When we feel defeated,
we need only take a deep breath
and say, 'Yes,'
and hope will reappear."

-- E. M. Forster (1879 - 1970)
English author

We need to take part in positive interactions both for ourselves and for others. We all win when we nurture a positive outlook. Nurturing positivity in ourselves and in others builds our resilience to setbacks.

(Photo by Gary Walker-Jones)

Also important is focusing on details and situations that are within our control. Trying to control anything outside of this realm merely creates frustration for everyone involved.

Allow others to control their details and situations, just as you would expect them to do for you. This is one way to contribute to the well-being of others.

*"Though you are disappointed,
there is hope.
Never let hope fail you!
Though one door is shut,
there are thousands still open to you."*

-- Friedrich Ruckert (1788 - 1866)
German poet & language professor

(Photo by Galina Nelyubova)

Throughout our lives, engaging in acts of kindness creates additional win-win scenarios. There are no losers when we are kind.

Nurturing

We can also express hope when we are alone, but our hopes grow exponentially when we surround ourselves with supportive or like-minded people. There are plenty of naysayers in the world. Adding supportive people to our personal circles adds to our strength, confidence, and resiliency.

(Photo by Joshua Hoehne)

"Don't be distracted by criticism. Remember, the only taste of success some people get is to take a bite out of you."

— Zig Ziglar (1926 – 2012)
American author & motivational speaker

Hope

(Photo by Jacob Morch)

8

Celebrating

> *"The reward of a thing well done is to have done it."*
>
> -- Ralph Waldo Emerson (1803 – 1882)
> American essayist, lecturer, abolitionist, & poet

Celebrations enhance our self-esteem. Having successful achievement acknowledged also builds our resilience by reenforcing our confidence and ability to persevere and overcome challenges.

We all appreciate a little recognition when we reach a goal. When our morale feels boosted, positive behavior is reinforced. We feel motivated to achieve future goals. Better still, our success thinking develops.

We know that Dopamine, the "happy chemical," is released in our brains. This happens when we close in on or achieve a goal. When our brains are happy, we are encouraged to continue positive actions.

*"Life affords no higher pleasure than that of
surmounting difficulties,
passing from one step of success to another,
forming new wishes,
and seeing them gratified.
He that labors
in any great or laudable undertaking
has his fatigues first supported by hope,
and afterwards rewarded by joy."*

-- Samuel Johnson (1709 - 1784)
English author, poet & playwright

(Photo by Ben White)

In groups, accolades and celebrations encourage team member connections and reinforce desired behaviors. Productivity increases. Collaboration and empathy are fostered. When we know we have done well, our productivity improves, and our successful mindset becomes positively boosted.

(Pablo Heimplatz)

"Success is not final; failure is not fatal: It is the courage to continue that counts."

— Winston Churchill (1874 – 1965)
British statesman, military officer, and writer
Prime Minister for the United Kingdom

We are experienced at celebrating big successes, like graduating, getting married, receiving a hard-earned job promotion, and more. However, reaching long-term goals takes time. We can get tired.

Recognizing our progress needs to include acknowledgement of even the smallest victories. Recognition of interim accomplishments gives us satisfaction and helps our overall happiness. We can keep big wins coming by celebrating the little wins. Recognizing even our small victories builds momentum and positively clarifies direction.

(Photo by Wout Vanacker)

Celebrating

To again reference our earlier example of a long-term weight loss goal, setting and meeting mini or interim goals also needs our acknowledgement. Perhaps we got up earlier on three mornings to exercise. This is a win because we had only gotten up early to exercise on one morning the previous week. Or maybe we chose a salad for lunch instead of our usual favorite pasta or bulky sandwich with fries. This is good. We are learning to eat healthier.

We can reward ourselves with something unrelated to food. Perhaps we would like some new workout gear or to take a dance class. Maybe we would enjoy a planned morning on which we will sleep in later or take in a movie or concert or comedy night.

(Photo by Shayna Douglas)

Celebrations could be a few minutes of self-time to read, relax, or enjoy nature. Even simply crossing items off our To Do lists is rewarding! Any nice, reward (non-caloric for weight loss) helps encourage our consistent and persistent positive behavior.

Interim goals are important. Small goals become building blocks for big success.

"Success is not the key to happiness. Happiness is the key to success. If you love what you are doing, you will be successful."

— Albert Schweitzer (1875 – 1965)
German French polymath

Our goals need to be attainable goals. We do not want to set ourselves up for failure by deciding that we want something that is very likely out of our reach.

For example, if I am a 75-year-old woman who has no on-stage musical experience or theatrical background, I probably would be reaching too far to suggest that I would like to star in a Broadway musical. Or, if I am a middle-aged man with a large beer belly, setting my sights on a high-fashion career as a runway model is far-fetched.

On the other hand, if we want to learn to cook, we can. A mini milestone might be growing from preparing omelets to making a quiche from scratch. We do not have to set a goal to become a master chef at a Michelin-starred restaurant.

Setting, working toward, and reaching goals can be fun. We need to enjoy the journey, not just the destination.

(Photo by Mario Dobelmann)

As we start planning the paths we want to follow to reach goals, it helps when we can stay focused. We need to clear our minds to concentrate better. This typically means removing distractions, such as computers, games, TV, and cell phones.

Depending on our overall, long-term goals, we could consider setting some weekly, monthly, or even quarterly goals. Such smaller, interim goals help prevent an annual goal from appearing overwhelming or unattainable.

(Photo by Levi Guzman)

Whatever our goals or timelines, we always want to celebrate our little successes. If we forget to celebrate, we risk burning out and decreasing our motivation and well-being.

(Photo by Pablo de la Fuente)

"Success breeds success."

– Aristotle (384 BC – 322 BC)
Greek philosopher & polymath
Popularized by William Durant (1885 – 1981)
American writer, historian, & philosopher
Often quoted by Mia Hamm (1972 -)
American professional soccer player

9

Worksheets

Writing down our thoughts, observations, and goals helps us clarify our thinking and makes our objectives more attainable. Create some pages that will become worksheets to strengthen Hope in your life and the lives of those around you.

Let's start with Positive Self Thoughts. First, list things you may recall hearing other people say about you. These can be as simple as recognition that you have a nice smile or a fun personality. They may be recent recollections or come from years ago.

Do not feel pressured to write dozens of items. Simply jot things down as you think of them. Perhaps just note one or two for now. Come back to your list and add more as often as you want. You may be surprised to "learn" just how wonderful you truly are.

Positive Self Thoughts
Nice Things Others Have Said:

1.
2.
3.
4.
5.
6.
7.
8.
9.
10.
11.
12.
13.
14.

Next, reflect on attributes that we may know or have known about ourselves. We may be aware that we always try to be kind to people, for example. Perhaps we were good at a sport when we were younger. Maybe we are particularly compassionate about animals, especially those in need.

<u>Positive Self Thoughts</u>
Things You Have Thought About You:

1.

2.

3.

4.

5.

6.

7.

8.

9.

10.

Next, let's focus on some Primary Goals. List one or two that have our highest priority. We can also list some secondary goals. These are goals that are on our radar, but they are not first on our mind.

Primary Goals

1.

2.

3.

Secondary Goals

1.

2.

3.

Worksheets

As we recall, attaining our big goals is helped by setting and accomplishing smaller steps on the way to big victories. Think about each primary and secondary goal. Jot down some of the interim points that, once reached, will also serve to bolster our progress toward bigger goals.

Big Goal:

1.

2.

3.

4.

5.

Big Goal:

1.

2.

3.

4.

5.

Success Rewards to Consider:
Remember to plan some little celebrations as we attain those interim goals. These do not need to be expensive nor time-consuming rewards. Think of the things that are personally motivating. They may not be incentives to someone else. These are personal pats on the back. Such mini motivators may be as simple as flowers, a comedy show, or a bubble bath.

Rewards for Interim Goal Attainment:

1.

2.

3.

4.

5.

Personal Nurturing Steps:

Self-care is vital. Without our mental, physical, and emotional well-being, little else can help us prepare for success. We do not want false hopes. We want to be the very best that we can possibly be.

Make a list of nurturing actions that we want and will commit to doing to become our best selves. Include a wide variety of items such as spending quality time with friends and family, taking nutritional supplements, engaging in activities that add knowledge, participating in programs that boost abilities for a favorite past-time or hobby, prioritizing good sleep habits, or practicing mindfulness through meditation or some other calming activity.

We all know ourselves and our needs. This is a personal list, not a place to write down what we think someone else wants us to do.

Physical Activity:

Healthy Eating:

Emotional Wellness:

Mental Growth:

9

In Closing

*"It is difficult to say what is impossible,
for the dream of yesterday is the hope of today
and the reality of tomorrow."*

-- Robert H. Goddard (1882 - 1945)
American physicist & inventor

An optimist is more hopeful than others, but even pessimists can be hopeful about some things. Hope makes us fuller people, happier people, inspired people.

(Photo by Casey Horner)

"Great hopes make great people."

-- Thomas Fuller (1608 - 1661)
English clergyman, historian, & author

(Photo by Kane Nori)

There is always hope. There are always reasons for hope. Morning will follow the night. Somebody is going to do something that somebody else said was impossible to do. Doers turn the impossible into the possible.

"True hope dwells on the possible, even when life seems to be a plot written by someone who wants to see how much adversity we can overcome."

-- Walter Inglis Anderson (1903 - 1976)
American painter & writer

Unrealistic expectations translate into false hope. This does not mean we should aim low. Hope needs to be grounded in realism, but let's aim for the stars. We won't touch them, but we won't come up with handfuls of mud either.

(Photo by Nicole Rose)

Hope

"We must accept finite disappointment but never lose infinite hope."

-- Martin Luther King, Jr.
(born Michael King, Jr.) (1929 – 1968)
American Baptist minister & civil rights activist
Assassinated by a radical Democrat in 1968

We need to believe in ourselves and always keep a little hope on hand. Hope is a key ingredient in a meaningful life. Hope is one of our Life Seasonings that is perfect all the time. It goes with everything. When we share hope with others, our own hope grows even stronger.

Photography Credits

Thank you to everyone who entrusted me with the use of their beautiful photographs.

Majid Akbari
Mohammad Alizade
J. Avard
Leopold Boettcher
Marko Brecic
Julia Caesar
Mark Casey
Eugene Chystekov
Demiahl
Pablo de la Fuente
Mario Dobelmann
Shayna Douglas
Julius Drost
Joshua Earle
Nick Fewings
Sasha Freemind
Graddes
Levi Guzman
Ahmed Hasan
Corey Hearne
Pablo Heimplatz
Joshua Hoehne
Casey Horner
Oleg Ivanov

Mark-Olivier Jodain
Endri Killo
Xandar Lacy
Yanis Ladjouzi
Jacob Morch
Nick Morrison
Hayley Murray
Galina Nelyubova
Siegfried Poepperl
Icha Rizkina
Nicole Rose
Alex Shute
Gavin Spear
Annie Spratt
Ryan Stone
Andrey Tikhanovskiy
Gabin Vallat
Wout Vanacker
Everton Vila
Klemen Vrankar
Anthony Wade
Gary Walker-Jones
Ben White

Special thanks to M. Rugesh Shah
for the cover photo.

Hope

(Cover photo by M. Rugesh Shah)

About the Author

Cathy Burnham Martin's first published work came in elementary school when an early poem won a town library contest. That was back when her parents refused to let her have the then-popular "Chatty Cathy" doll, stating that one chatty Cathy in the house was more than enough. Though poetry took a back seat, she drove her writing and blabbing proficiencies along a highly eclectic career path through college recruitment, telecom marketing, corporate communications, TV broadcasting with an ABC affiliate, station management of an award-winning PEG-access station, bank organizing, and investor relations. An active board member and volunteer, she received Easter Seals' David P. Goodwin Lifetime Commitment Award. This professional voiceover artist, humorist, musical actress, journalist, and dedicated foodie earned numerous awards as a news anchor and businesswoman. She has produced and hosted groundbreaking documentaries, TV specials, and news reports, from the Moscow Superpower Summit and the opening of the Berlin Wall to coverage of Presidential Primaries. A born storyteller and business speaker dubbed "The Morale Booster," Cathy is a member of Actors Equity and writes daily articles for social media and the GoodLiving123.com website.

Other Titles

Life Seasonings series:
  Perspectives

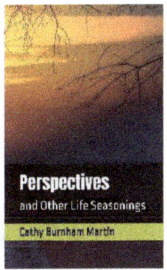

The Destiny trilogy:
  Destiny of Dreams… Time Is Dear
  Destiny of Determination… Faith and Family
  Destiny of Daring… Never Forget

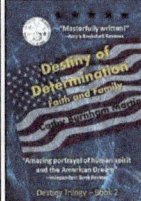

A Dangerous Book for Dogs:
  Train Your Humans with the Bandit Method
Dog Days in the Life of the Miles-Mannered Man

Healthy Thinking Habits:
   Seven Attitude Skills Simplified
Good Living Skills: Learned from My Mother
Encouragement: How to Be and Find Your Best

Of the Same Blood: Your Eurasian Heritage
The Ronald…
   Daydreams, Wonderments & Other Ponderings

The Bimbo Has Brains… and Other Freaky Facts
The Bimbo Has MORE Brains…
   Surviving Political Correctness

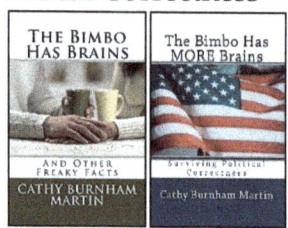

From the KISS Keep It Super Simple cookbooks:

50 Years of Fabulous Family Favorites
   Sippers, Starters, and Sweets
   Lunch, Brunch, and Entrees
   Sides, Soup, Salad, Snacks, Etc.

Champagne! Facts, Fizz, Food, & Fun
Cranberry Cooking

Dockside Dining: (series)
   Round One
   A Second Helping
   Back for Thirds

Lobacious Lobster…
 Decadently Super Simple Recipes

Find all books by Cathy Burnham Martin in paperback, digital, and audiobook formats anywhere books are sold and on her **www.GoodLiving123.com** site.

Partial List of Audiobooks Narrated by Cathy Burnham Martin

Fiction
Destiny Trilogy:
    Destiny of Dreams… Time Is Dear
      (Violent content warning)
    Destiny of Determination… Faith and Family
    Destiny of Daring… Never Forget
A Dangerous Book for Dogs…
    Train Your Humans with the Bandit Method
Kremlins Trilogy (Violent content warning)
    Citadels of Fire
    Bastions of Blood
    Dungeons of Destiny:
        An Epic Russian Historical Romance
Daniel's Fork: A Mystery Set in the
        Daniel's Fork Universe
            (Adult content warning)
The Relentless Brit

Non-Fiction

Encouragement: How to Be and Find the Best
Good Living Skills… Learned from My Mother
Healthy Thinking Habits:
    Seven Attitude Skills Simplified
The Bimbo Has Brains: And Other Freaky Facts
The Bimbo Has MORE Brains:
    Surviving Political Correctness
31 Days to a Stronger Marriage:
    A Guide to Building Closer Relationships
Exploring Past Lives: A Guide to the Soul's Travels
Why We Fail in Love: A Study into the Pursuit of
    One of Mankind's Most Precious Desires
The Hormone Fix: Naturally Rebalance Your System
    in 10 Weeks

www.ingramcontent.com/pod-product-compliance
Lightning Source LLC
Chambersburg PA
CBHW060359050426
42449CB00009B/1811